English Foundation

Activity Book C

T0318140

Published by Collins
An imprint of HarperCollins*Publishers*
The News Building, 1 London Bridge Street,
London, SE1 9GF, UK

HarperCollins*Publishers*
Macken House, 39/40 Mayor Street Upper,
Dublin 1, DO1 C9W8, Ireland

Browse the complete Collins catalogue at
www.collins.co.uk

© HarperCollins*Publishers* Limited 2021

10 9 8 7 6 5 4 3

ISBN 978-0-00-846859-0

British Library Cataloguing-in-Publication Data
A catalogue record for this publication is available from the British Library.

Author: Fiona Macgregor
Publisher: Elaine Higgleton
Product manager: Letitia Luff
Commissioning editor: Rachel Houghton
Edited by: Hannah Hirst-Dunton
Editorial management: Oriel Square
Cover designer: Kevin Robbins
Cover illustrations: Jouve India Pvt Ltd.
Internal illustrations: Jouve India Pvt. Ltd.,
p 2 David Hill, p 11–14 Beccy Blake,
p 15 Q2Amedia, p 19 Tasneem Amiruddin
Typesetter: Jouve India Pvt. Ltd.
Production controller: Lyndsey Rogers
Printed and Bound in the UK using 100% Renewable
Electricity at Martins the Printers

Acknowledgements

With thanks to all the kindergarten staff and their schools around the world who have helped with the development of this course, by sharing insights and commenting on and testing sample materials:

Calcutta International School: Sharmila Majumdar, Mrs Pratima Nayar, Preeti Roychoudhury, Tinku Yadav, Lakshmi Khanna, Mousumi Guha, Radhika Dhanuka, Archana Tiwari, Urmita Das; Gateway College (Sri Lanka): Kousala Benedict; Hawar International School: Kareen Barakat, Shahla Mohammed, Jennah Hussain; Manthan International School: Shalini Reddy; Monterey Pre-Primary: Adina Oram; Prometheus School: Aneesha Sahni, Deepa Nanda; Pragyanam School: Monika Sachdev; Rosary Sisters High School: Samar Sabat, Sireen Freij, Hiba Mousa; Solitaire Global School: Devi Nimmagadda; United Charter Schools (UCS): Tabassum Murtaza and staff; Vietnam Australia International School: Holly Simpson

The publishers wish to thank the following for permission to reproduce photographs.

(t = top, c = centre, b = bottom, r = right, l = left)

p 7tl yampi/Shutterstock, p 7tr Jiang Hongyan/Shutterstock p 7cl1 yampi/Shutterstock, p 7cr1 everydayplus/Shutterstock, p 7cl1 yampi/Shutterstock, p 7cr2 noprati somchit/Shutterstock, p 7bl yampi/Shutterstock, p 7br Pakmor/Shutterstock, p 9t yampi/Shutterstock, p 9c1 yampi/Shutterstock, p 9c2 Seregam/Shutterstock

The publishers gratefully acknowledge the permission granted to reproduce the copyright material in this book. Every effort has been made to trace copyright holders and to obtain their permission for the use of copyright material. The publishers will gladly receive any information enabling them to rectify any error or omission at the first opportunity.

Extracts from Collins Big Cat readers reprinted by permission of HarperCollins *Publishers* Ltd

All © HarperCollins*Publishers*

MIX
Paper | Supporting
responsible forestry
FSC™ C007454

This book is produced from independently certified FSC™ paper to ensure responsible forest management.

For more information visit:
www.harpercollins.co.uk/green

Put in order

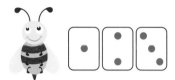

1 2 3 4 5 6

Put the pictures in order. Number them
1, 2, 3, 4, 5 and 6.   Date:

Circle

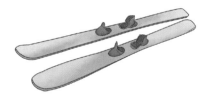

Circle the things you need in the rain.

Date:

Colour and say

Colour the things you need on a sunny day.
Say what you can see.   Date:

Draw

Monday	Tuesday
Wednesday	**Thursday**
Friday	**Saturday**

Draw the weather for this week.

Date:

Trace and say

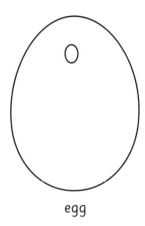

egg

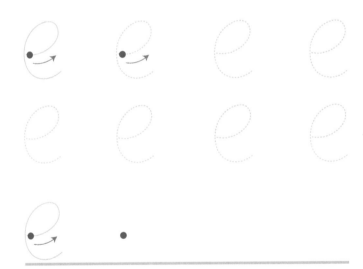

Trace the letter. Say the sound. Colour in the picture.

Date:

Match

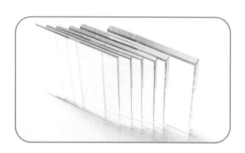

Match the things to the materials they are made of.

Date:

Draw

| table | window | bed | wall |

Draw a room with a table, a window,
a bed and a wall.

Date:

Trace and say

W

W

W

W

W all

W indow

W ood

W eather

Trace the pattern. Complete the words.
Say them out loud.   Date:

Trace

Trace over the dotted lines to finish the pictures.

Date:

Follow

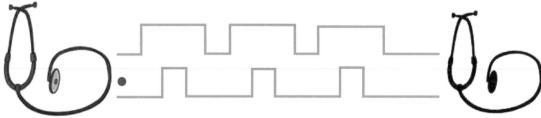

Draw a line along the path from each picture to its shadow. Start at the red dot.

Date:

11

Match

Match the jobs to the objects.

Date:

Trace and say

t t t t

t t t t

t

p p p p

p p p p

p

teacher

postman

Trace the letters. Say the sounds. What jobs do these people do?

Date:

Trace and say

d d d d
d d d d
d

doctor

b b b b
b b b b
b

builder

Trace the letters. Say the sounds. What jobs do these people do?

Date:

Find

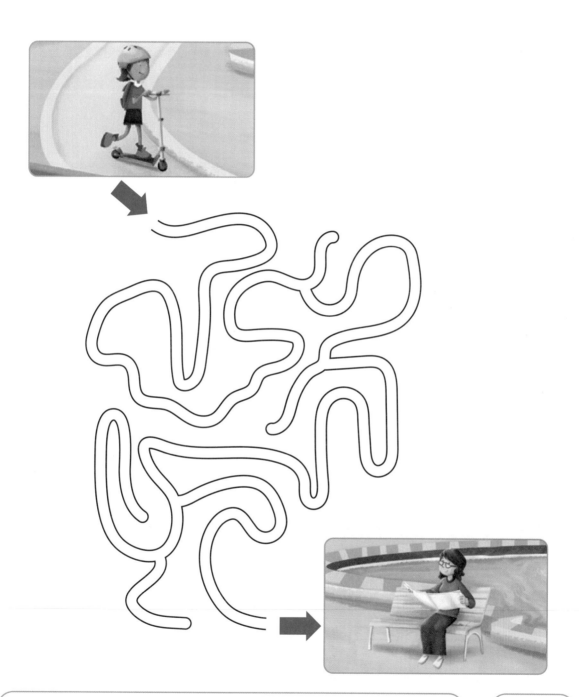

Help the girl to find her mum.

Date:

Find

in	on	under

Find the bees. Use the words in the box to say where they are.

Date:

over

behind

in front of

Circle

Circle the things you have at home.

Date:

Colour

Colour the trucks blue. Colour the cars red.
Colour the motorbikes yellow.

Date:

19

Find and circle

    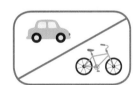

Follow the pattern in each line.
Circle what comes next.   Date:

Draw

Draw your favourite technology.

Date:

Alphabet time

rabbit

sun

table

umbrella

Alongside structured phonics lessons, you may want to display and talk about one letter of the alphabet in an 'alphabet time' session each week.

Alphabet time

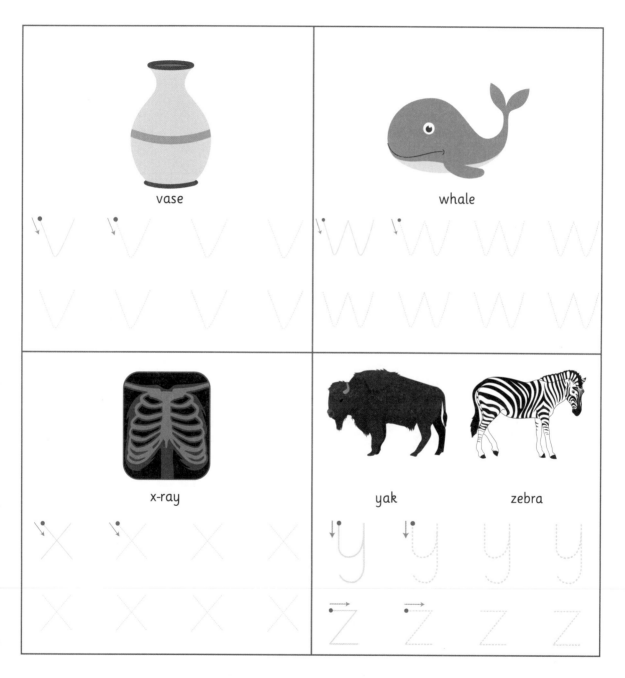

vase

whale

x-ray

yak

zebra

Alongside structured phonics lessons, you may want to display and talk about one letter of the alphabet in an 'alphabet time' session each week.

Assessment record

_____ has achieved these English Foundation Phase Objectives:

Reading

R1 Become aware of sound structures in language	1	2	3
R2 Develop pre-reading skills	1	2	3
R3 Recognise some letters of the English alphabet	1	2	3
R4 Understand and explore the link between letters and the sounds they represent	1	2	3
Reading motor skills	1	2	3

Writing

W1 Develop pre-writing skills	1	2	3
Writing motor skills	1	2	3

Speaking

S1 Be able to express oneself in everyday situations	1	2	3
S2 Understand sentences	1	2	3
Speaking developmental skills	1	2	3

Listening

L1 Know how to listen and respond appropriately in everyday contexts	1	2	3
Listening developmental skills	1	2	3

1: Partially achieved
2: Achieved
3: Exceeded

Signed by teacher:
Signed by parent:

Date: